972.92   Jamaica in pictures.
JAM

$19.95   11BT01639

DATE			

G R CLARK JR SR HG
1921 DAVIS AVE
WHITING, IN 46394

BAKER & TAYLOR

JAMAICA

…in Pictures

Visual Geography Series®

JAMAICA

...in Pictures

Prepared by
Geography Department

Lerner Publications Company
Minneapolis

Courtesy of Inter-American Development Bank

Jamaicans often run small craft businesses from their homes — as this man does, using straw to make baskets.

This book is an all-new edition of the Visual Geography Series. Previous editions have been published by Sterling Publishing Company, New York City. The text, set in 10/12 Century Textbook, is fully revised and updated, and new photographs, maps, charts, and captions have been added.

LIBRARY OF CONGRESS CATALOGING-IN-PUBLICATION DATA

Jamaica in pictures.

(Visual geography series)
Rev. ed. of: Jamaica in pictures / by Anne Egan.
Includes index.
Summary: Text and photographs present Jamaica's history, government, land, economy, and people.
1. Jamaica. [1. Jamaica] I. Egan, Anne. Jamaica in pictures. II. Lerner Publications Company. Geography Dept. III. Title. IV. Series: Visual geography series (Minneapolis, Minn.)
F1868.J263   1987   972.92   86-33817
ISBN 0-8225-1814-7 (lib. bdg.)

International Standard Book Number: 0-8225-1814-7
Library of Congress Catalog Card Number: 86-33817

VISUAL GEOGRAPHY SERIES®

Publisher
Harry Jonas Lerner
Associate Publisher
Nancy M. Campbell
Senior Editor
Mary M. Rodgers
Editor
Gretchen Bratvold
Editorial Assistant
Nora W. Kniskern
Illustrations Editor
Nathan A. Haverstock
Karen A. Sirvaitis
Consultants/Contributors
Dr. Ruth F. Hale
Nathan A. Haverstock
Sandra K. Davis
Designer
Jim Simondet
Cartographer
Carol F. Barrett
Indexer
Kristine S. Schubert
Production Manager
Gary J. Hansen

Independent Picture Service

Rafting near Kingston on the tranquil Ferry River is an excellent way to see the Jamaican backcountry.

Acknowledgments

Title page photo courtesy of Jamaica Tourist Board.

Elevation contours adapted from *The Times Atlas of the World,* seventh comprehensive edition (New York: Times Books, 1985).

5 6 7 8 9 10 – JR – 02 01 00 99 98 97

Nestled in the foothills of the famed mountain range from which it gets its name, the Blue Mountain Inn is Kingston's most renowned restaurant.

Contents

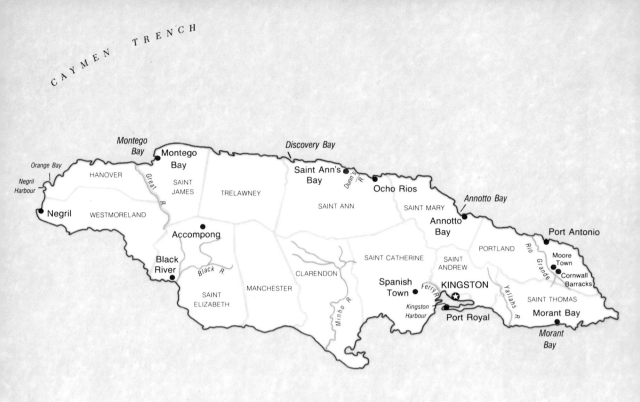

CAYMEN TRENCH

Orange Bay

Negril Harbour

Montego Bay

Discovery Bay

HANOVER

SAINT JAMES

TRELAWNEY

Great R.

Montego Bay

Negril

WESTMORELAND

Accompong

Black River

Black R.

SAINT ELIZABETH

MANCHESTER

CLARENDON

Minho R.

SAINT ANN

Saint Ann's Bay

Dunn's R.

Ocho Rios

SAINT MARY

SAINT CATHERINE

Spanish Town

Ferry R.

Kingston Harbour

Annotto Bay

SAINT ANDREW

KINGSTON

Port Royal

Annotto Bay

PORTLAND

Rio Grande

Port Antonio

Moore Town

Cornwall Barracks

Yallahs R.

SAINT THOMAS

Morant Bay

Morant Bay

CARIBBEAN SEA

JAMAICA

N

Parish Boundaries

0   20 Miles

0   20 Kilometers

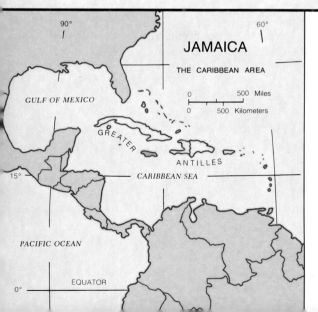

90°   60°

JAMAICA

THE CARIBBEAN AREA

0   500 Miles

0   500 Kilometers

GULF OF MEXICO

GREATER

ANTILLES

CARIBBEAN SEA

15°

PACIFIC OCEAN

0°

EQUATOR

METRIC CONVERSION CHART
To Find Approximate Equivalents

WHEN YOU KNOW:	MULTIPLY BY:	TO FIND:
AREA		
acres	0.41	hectares
square miles	2.59	square kilometers
CAPACITY		
gallons	3.79	liters
LENGTH		
feet	30.48	centimeters
yards	0.91	meters
miles	1.61	kilometers
MASS (weight)		
pounds	0.45	kilograms
tons	0.91	metric tons
VOLUME		
cubic yards	0.77	cubic meters
TEMPERATURE		
degrees Fahrenheit	0.56 (*after* subtracting 32)	degrees Celsius

With Jamaica's abundance of fresh fruit and vegetables, food arranging becomes an art. Here, papaya is served in a bowl, surrounded by a banana, hibiscus flowers, purple star apples, and a red, pear-shaped Otaheite apple.

Introduction

With independence from Great Britain in 1962, the island nation of Jamaica set about redefining itself. By blending relevant traditions of the past with newer institutions, Jamaicans have begun to create a new society.

For example, in an attempt to redistribute the nation's wealth more equally among its citizens, the Jamaican government dissolved the old planter aristocracy. The unjust system had been imposed by the British during three centuries of colonial rule. Some other British institutions, however—including the basic form of government and excellent public schools —were maintained. This continuity has helped successive government administra-

tions—though sharply divided on the direction of the nation—to work out their differences within a democratic context.

About 96 percent of Jamaica's people are of African or part-African origins, and the black majority exercises power with fairness to all—including the 4 percent of East Indian, Chinese, or European origin. Together all Jamaicans are trying to live up to their nation's motto: "Out of Many, One People."

Jamaica has long attracted vacationers from the United States because of the rich and varied beauty of the land—sandy beaches, clear rivers, brilliantly colored tropical flora, and a mountainous interior that is cool and refreshing. Visitors to the

Kingston, the capital of Jamaica, is the nation's largest metropolis and commercial port.

island can also learn about the country's rich cultural traditions.

Jamaicans have launched new theater and dance companies, which bring to worldwide audiences Jamaican art forms that spring from African roots. Jamaicans have also originated a new religion, Rastafarianism, which looks to the African nation of Ethiopia as the Promised Land.

Though flourishing culturally, Jamaica has encountered substantial obstacles to economic self-sufficiency. The unemployment rate is high, and many Jamaicans have gone abroad—to Great Britain, the United States, or elsewhere in the Caribbean—in search of jobs.

Recent years have brought a steep decline in Jamaica's earnings from bauxite (from which aluminum is made), owing to a global oversupply of this raw product. Bauxite once generated two-thirds of the country's export earnings. Today bauxite is sold for less than it costs to produce, and workers are underpaid.

Port Antonio's Blue Lagoon, reputed to be bottomless, attracts tourists and water-sports enthusiasts.

Jamaica's bauxite workers are under-paid, in part because profits from exports of the ore are decreasing.

With an annual inflation rate of more than 50 percent in the early 1990s, Jamaican workers have used strikes to express their dissatisfaction over the decrease in the value of their paychecks. At the insistence of the United States, Jamaica has cracked down hard on the growing of marijuana—a crop whose illegal profits have helped offset declines in other legal areas of the economy.

But despite these problems, Jamaicans are proud of the strides their country has taken to achieve racial equality. Jamaicans believe equality is the best guarantee that they will be able to retain their recently achieved independence.

With U.S. assistance, Jamaica has trained a special force to curtail the production of the illegal drug marijuana.

Courtesy of Kathleen Rosow

The Blue Mountains are nearly always wrapped in clouds, but on a clear day hikers and other explorers can see most of the eastern half of the island.

1) The Land

Jamaica, an island in the Caribbean Sea, lies 480 miles south of Florida. With 4,471 square miles of territory, the landmass is slightly smaller than the state of Connecticut. Approached by sea, Jamaica resembles a great tropical iceberg, with about two-thirds of its surface lying below the water, while the remaining one-third juts raggedly into the air. The third largest island in the Caribbean, Jamaica is approximately 145 miles long and 53 miles wide at its farthest points.

Jamaica is a land of scenic beauty and variety. Mountains, fern forests, open plains, beaches, plateaus, rivers, and waterfalls give this sun-drenched, wind-swept island the appearance of a tropical paradise.

Geographical Setting

The Caribbean Sea, an arm of the Atlantic Ocean, encompasses the islands of Jamaica, Cuba, and the rest of the West Indies, also called the Greater Antilles. The Caribbean extends from the Florida Keys south to Venezuela, Colombia, Panama, and Costa Rica, and west to Nicaragua, Honduras, Guatemala, Belize, and Mexico.

When Columbus discovered the Caribbean, he thought the islands were the mythical land of Antillia, or the "Isles of the Blest." Jamaica, Cuba, Hispaniola (which contains the nations of Haiti and the Dominican Republic), and Puerto Rico form an island group known as the Greater Antilles, which is part of the Leeward Island chain. The Greater Antilles are believed to be the peaks of a once-extensive mountain range that may have been joined to the mainland of Central America but was eventually submerged. The Cayman Trench—the deepest point in the Caribbean Sea—forms a 24,720-foot-deep gulf between Jamaica and the tiny, British-ruled Cayman Islands to the west. The Lesser Antilles, named the Windward Islands because they lie in the direct path of the northeast trade winds, lie east and south of Puerto Rico.

Topography and Climate

From west to east in Jamaica runs a rugged highland chain, the Blue Mountains, whose highest peak is 7,388 feet. Farther to the

Courtesy of Jamaica Tourist Board

Coconut trees thrive in Jamaica's warm climate and, until recently, were an important source of products both for export and for local consumption. Many of these palms, however, have been wiped out by disease.

Courtesy of Kathleen Rosow

Aqueducts, once used to water Jamaica's plantations, still dot the countryside in the island's southern parishes.

east, a smaller range called the John Crow Mountains reaches an altitude of 3,800 feet. A large portion of the island consists of a limestone plateau that is pitted with sink-holes, caverns, hills, and valleys. Plains circle the island and separate the mountains from the sea. An estimated 200 rivers and streams and many small tributaries spill or trickle onto these plains from the hills. The island has several hot springs, as well as a lava cone that formed from volcanic activity.

Brushed by the trade winds, Jamaica is almost always balmy. The average annual temperature variation is only about 6° F. The capital city of Kingston averages 81.4° F in July and 76° F in January. The moderating influence of the sea keeps the lowland temperatures from exceeding 91° F and from falling below 60° F. The highlands may have an occasional light frost, but the average temperature is in the low seventies. Temperature variation affects the crop pattern on the island. In

Courtesy of Kevin L. Olsen

Small-scale farmers have leveled terraces of land to raise crops in the Blue Mountains.

Courtesy of Jamaica Tourist Board

The beach at Ocho Rios on Jamaica's north coast is a center for international tourists.

Hurricanes threaten the island during the rainy season, when coconut palms bend nearly double under the occasional torrents of rain carried by the northeast trade winds. Such storms can severely disrupt the economy. For example, Hurricane Gilbert destroyed crops, hotels, and residences when it struck Jamaica in 1988.

The lighthouse at Port Antonio helps guide ships through stormy weather.

the mountains, farmers grow potatoes, coffee, and strawberries. In the lowlands, coconuts and sugarcane thrive.

Like all tropical islands, Jamaica has a rainy season, which begins in April and brings the heaviest precipitation in September, October, and November. Since the prevailing winds blow from the northeast, that area of the island receives the most rainfall—nearly 100 inches a year—while the southeastern coast receives only about 35 inches. Inland, the peaks of the Blue Mountains receive more than 200 inches of rain a year and are nearly always wrapped in soft clouds. During hurricanes and throughout the rainy season, floods and landslides damage roads throughout the island. Crews of road workers frequently patch and bolster up the washed-out sections. The rugged nature of the terrain makes road building a problem, but the roads are in relatively good condition despite these hazards.

13

The colorful hibiscus grows wild in Jamaica's countryside.

The John Crow, with its excellent eyesight, scavenges for food from extremely high altitudes.

Flora and Fauna

Jamaican vegetation is colorful and varied. Many of the plants, shrubs, and trees found on the island have been brought from other places throughout the centuries. Bananas, sugarcane, coffee, tobacco, coconuts, allspice, bamboo, ackee, nutmeg, breadfruit, and tamarind thrive on farms, and rampant growths of poinsettia, hibiscus, poinciana, oleander, and bougainvillea cover the countryside.

One of the most extraordinary trees is the ceiba, with palmlike leaves and large, bell-shaped flowers. Often growing taller than 130 feet and living for hundreds of years, these trees are regarded with superstition and awe. Also known as the silk-cotton tree, the ceiba has seeds that contain a silky floss used as insulation or as stuffing for pillows and furniture. For centuries fishermen have used the trunks of the ceibas to make dugout canoes.

Only one native mammal—the coney, or wild rabbit—survives among Jamaica's wildlife. The mongoose was brought in from India in 1872 to exterminate snakes and rats. As a result, few snakes exist in Jamaica, and none are poisonous. Liz-

Anthurium, a tropical plant with highly colored leaves, is displayed in a Jamaican market.

Catching land crabs along the island's many rivers is a popular pastime in Jamaica. This man displays his catch, which will be eaten for dinner.

ards—harmless and amusing to watch— are abundant. The island has at least 200 varieties of birds. Jamaican nightingales, hummingbirds, parrots, swallows, thrushes, woodpeckers, doves, and owls are a few of the many birds. Spindle-legged sandpip- ers are commonly seen running along the beaches. River crocodiles provide game for sportspeople, as do the abundant tarpon, wahoo, marlin, and sailfish in the deep waters off the coast. Oysters, lobsters, and shrimp are also plentiful.

This huge marlin was caught during one of the marlin tournaments that are held each year at Port Antonio on Jamaica's northeastern coast.

Kingston—Jamaica's capital city—is situated between the Blue Mountains and the sea. Built on an excellent harbor, this active commercial center is the largest English-speaking city south of Miami, Florida.

The Parishes

Jamaica is divided into 14 parishes, each one different from the next. The capital of each parish—with its own local government, church, and market—is the hub of activity for the rest of that parish.

SOUTHERN SHORES

Jamaica's southern shore was the first major area of settlement by Spanish colonists. In what is now the parish of Saint Andrew, Port Royal was established as the first strategic point and port of trade. One of the most important cities in the New World, Port Royal was a favorite pirate haunt until its destruction by earthquake in 1692. Legend has it that Port Royal's fate was payment in kind for its criminal life as a center for pirates. Today, surrounded by an air of desolation, Port Royal is filled with relics of the past.

After the earthquake in 1692, a new port of entry was established at nearby Kingston, located in the parish of Kingston. In 1872 this city became the capital of the island. Situated on a very deep, large, and nearly landlocked arm of the sea, Kingston throbs with activity. The heart of business, trade, and culture, the city covers a 10-square-mile area, and with its entire

Modern structures line the shorefront in downtown Kingston, thanks to a building project begun in the 1960s.

metropolitan area has a population of nearly 600,000. Central Kingston is a maze of streets and back lanes. Despite the wreckage of earthquakes, hurricanes, and fires throughout its history, Kingston has been reconstructed after each disaster, creating a mix of architecture from old colonial to modern. Vale Royal, one of the most beautiful of Jamaica's historic great houses, or plantation homes, was built in 1694. It is now the official home of Jamaica's prime minister.

Courtesy of Jamaica Tourist Board

Vale Royal, the official residence of the prime minister, has deep porches set off by Victorian-era decoration.

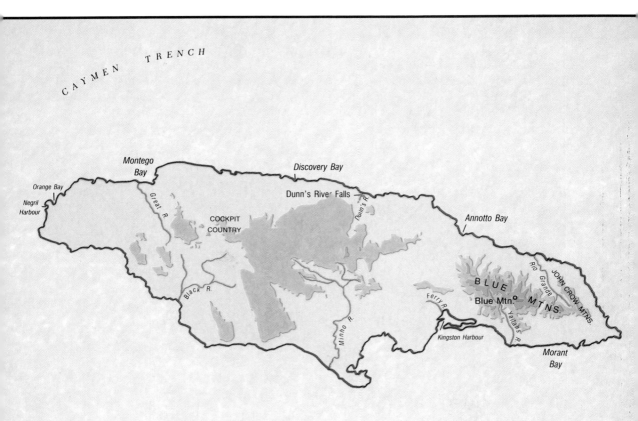

CAYMEN TRENCH

Montego Bay

Discovery Bay

Orange Bay

Negril Harbour

Great R.

Dunn's River Falls

Dunn's R.

Annotto Bay

COCKPIT COUNTRY

Rio Grande

JOHN CROW MTNS.

Black R.

B L U E

Blue Mtn.

M T N S.

Ferry R.

Minho R.

Yallahs R.

Kingston Harbour

Morant Bay

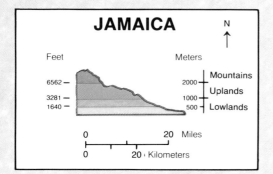

JAMAICA

N

Feet		Meters	
		2000	Mountains
6562			Uplands
3281		1000	
1640		500	Lowlands

0   20   Miles

0   20   Kilometers

CARIBBEAN SEA

Other parishes along Jamaica's southern shore include Saint Catherine, Clarendon, Manchester, and Saint Elizabeth. Columbus made his first contact with the Arawak Indians on the coast of Clarendon. Early Spanish settlers panned for gold in Clarendon's Minho River. Richly fertile, this parish was the heart of plantation life. Farther west, at Black River in the parish of Saint Elizabeth, the air is humid and equatorial—like no other place in Jamaica. Yellow fever and malaria plagued early colonists in this area.

THE EAST

Bounded on the west by the twisting Yallahs River, the parish of Saint Thomas forms the southeastern tip of Jamaica. Here, at Morant Bay, was the scene of a historic slave rebellion in 1865, and evidence of those stormy times can still be seen. Storms of another kind—hurricanes—fiercely lash this coastal area, more so than any other part of the island.

To the north is the parish of Portland, on whose border rises Blue Mountain—Jamaica's highest peak. The shores of Portland are among the most popular tourist areas on the island. One resort, Port Antonio, lies at the mouth of one of the largest rivers in Jamaica—the Rio Grande—which is the scene of exciting rafting trips. The eastern coast is dotted with coconut palms that bend nearly double under the occasional sudden onset of the northeast trade winds—which spill great torrents of rain on the steeply rising slopes. Inland in the John Crow Mountains are two towns—Cornwall Barracks and Moore Town—that provided refuge for fugitive African slaves during the seventeenth and eighteenth centuries.

Independent Picture Service

In the parish of Saint Thomas, fishermen's boats and nets form an interesting design against the sky. Like the Arawaks centuries before them, fishermen of Jamaica often use the wood of the giant ceiba tree to make dugout canoes.

The town of **Port Antonio** *(above and left)* on the northeast coast retains a relaxed and peaceful charm despite its emergence as a major center of tourism.

Skilled boatmen pole long, bamboo rafts down the broad Rio Grande near Port Antonio. Once the rafts were used to bring bananas and produce from the mountains to the sea. Now, visitors enjoy the cool ride and the natural beauty of the lush rainforests.

Breeds of cattle from India have adapted to the climate and vegetation of Jamaica's lowlands, where both beef and dairy cattle are raised. Pasture grasses and crossbreeding techniques have been improved in an effort to develop the beef and dairy industries.

THE GOLD COAST

Known as the Gold Coast because of the growing tourist trade, the northern coast is made up of the parishes of Saint Mary, Saint Ann, Trelawney, and Saint James. In Saint Ann, lowlands and rolling hills support cattle and allspice estates. Christopher Columbus made his first landing on Jamaica in Saint Ann near Discovery Bay. Farther east in the same parish lies the town of Ocho Rios. Now a booming tourist center, Ocho Rios was originally called Las Chorreras, "The Waterfalls." A short distance away is Dunn's River Falls, whose cool waters spill directly onto one of the best bathing beaches on the island.

Columbus Park at Discovery Bay—located on the coast of the parish of Saint Ann—was developed to commemorate Columbus's first explorations of Jamaica in the late 1400s.

Trelawney is markedly different from its adjoining parishes. Although the coast is built up, the interior is part of the desolate Cockpit Country. A large segment of the limestone mass of the island is studded with alternating sinkholes (or craters) and mounds. Endless caverns lie underground and fascinate explorers. According to legend, the runaway slaves who discovered this wild haven had to keep looking over their shoulders to make sure they were not being followed—hence, it is known familiarly as the "Land of Look Behind."

Courtesy of Jamaica Tourist Board

Courtesy of Jamaica Tourist Board

The eerie, unusual landscape of the Cockpit Country *(above and left)* comprises 500 square miles within the parishes of Trelawney, Saint Elizabeth, and Saint James. Regarded as Jamaica's most inhospitable region, few roads cross the territory, and much of it remains unexplored.

Descendents of the early fugitive slaves, Maroon people live in the Cockpit Country and are believed to represent mixed African-and-Spanish ancestry.

Independent Picture Service

The famed Tyrall golf course, with Round Hill and Montego Bay in the background, is one of three championship courses on the island.

One of the main resort areas in the Caribbean is Montego Bay, in the parish of Saint James. Luxury hotels, private homes on a grand scale, and fashion houses have all turned this one-time plantation port into Jamaica's principal tourist center. The strains of calypso music and a lively nightlife lend an animated atmosphere to Montego Bay.

Nearby is Rose Hall—one of the most legendary houses in Jamaica. Here lived the "White Witch," Annie Palmer, who is reported to have done away with many of her lovers, using either poison or her own voodoo powers. She herself was found murdered in bed, and it is said her ghost still roams the great house. Jamaican writer George de Lisser has immortalized Mrs. Palmer in the historical novel *The White Witch of Rose Hall.*

Regarded as Jamaica's most magnificent great house (residence of a plantation owner), Rose Hall was built between 1770 and 1780. The house fell into ruin during the nineteenth century but has since been restored with period furnishings.

With almost 10 miles of rocky shore-line and beaches of pure white sand, Negril Harbour on the western end of the island is one of Jamaica's leading tourist spots – though far less formal than other resorts on the island.

A squatter – one who settles on property without having a legal title and without paying rent – has set up a makeshift farm in the dense, swamp-like area on the coast of Orange Bay, near Negril. Farming arrangements such as this can be found throughout the island.

THE WEST

The swampy, underdeveloped western shores of Jamaica are shared by the parishes of Hanover and Westmoreland. Although Hanover is both the smallest and the flattest parish on the island, its gently rounded hills afford views of the island and surrounding waters that are unmatched. One of the island's major rivers, the Great River, forms Hanover's eastern boundary with Saint James. Negril Harbour, which spans about 10 miles, begins in Hanover and extends into the parish of Westmoreland. Once known as Bloody Bay—probably because whales were butchered there—the marshy, secluded area of Negril is attractive to drug dealers. The scene of much pirate activity in centuries past, Negril more recently has been the site of oil drilling and tourism. The swampy conditions in some areas are ideal for rice production.

Jamaica, a British colony until 1962, adopted a bold new flag when independent status was gained. The flag's green triangles stand for agriculture and hope for the future, the yellow stripes stand for the sun, and the black triangles stand for the past—including the African heritage of the majority of Jamaica's people.

2) History and Government

On May 5, 1494, on his second trip to the New World, Christopher Columbus discovered Jamaica for Spain, thinking he had found a great mainland. Landing on the northern coast, he gave the name Santa Gloria—for its beauty—to the spot known today as Saint Ann's Bay. After traveling to Cuba, Columbus returned to Jamaica, where he thought there might be gold. Landing this time on the southern coast at Old Harbour, Columbus encountered the Arawaks—peace-loving Indians who had lived in Jamaica since prehistoric times.

The Arawaks

The Arawaks had avoided extermination at the hands of the fierce Carib Indians, who were conducting a large-scale conquest of the Caribbean at the time of the arrival of the Europeans. Following a peaceful way of life, the Arawaks avoided conflict. Excavations of the area have revealed theirs to be a Stone Age culture. Among the few reminders of Arawak life are some remnants of their pottery.

Most evidence indicates that the Arawaks were related to the Indians of Cen-

24

From cotton the Arawaks wove hammocks, which served as their principal item of furniture.

tral America, but their civilization bore no resemblance to the culture of the Aztecs and Maya in Central America. Leading a simple existence, the Arawaks depended on the sea that surrounded them. When the Spanish arrived, the Arawaks probably numbered about 70,000. By the seventeenth century, the Arawaks had been completely obliterated from the island. Unable to endure the physical hardship

The few remains of the Jamaican Arawaks include simple stone and metal implements, called celts, as well as fragments of pottery. Their principal tool was an axhead made of stone.

Independent Picture Service

This plaster cast of a birdman was made from an Arawak image found in a cave in Clarendon in 1792. The Arawaks, who arrived in Jamaica around A.D. 600, came to be a flourishing tribe with a simple but well-established culture. Skilled craftspeople, they carved bowls from wood and sculpted ceremonial objects from wood and stone.

and disease imposed by their Spanish and English conquerors, the Arawaks left little in their wake but the origin of the name for their island, *Xamayca* (Land of Wood and Water).

The Spanish

When Christopher Columbus first sighted Jamaica in 1494, he was on a mission for the Spanish crown to find both gold and a shorter route to the West Indies. He did not return to Jamaica until 1503—after an unsuccessful search for gold in Panama. On his way back to Cuba from Panama, Columbus was plagued by leaking ships and short supplies. He barely managed to reach Santa Gloria—his original landfall in Jamaica—on June 24, 1503. Because his

two ships were in such poor condition, the aging explorer was forced to remain in Jamaica for a year.

The year proved to be very difficult. Shortage of food was a constant problem, and the 116-man crew grew restless. Columbus's man-at-arms, Diego Mendez, set out in a canoe for nearby Hispaniola to seek aid. In his absence, Francisco Porras —along with 50 crew members who were enraged by the illness and food shortage that plagued them—staged a mutiny. Eventually the rebels were defeated by Columbus's brother Bartholomeo. The peaceful Arawaks were horrified at the combative behavior of the Spanish and refused to continue to bring them food and supplies.

Despite the cruel abuse of the Arawaks by some of the crew, Columbus sought to retain their respect and help. Pretending to be a god, he prophesied that the moon would disappear if the Indians failed to bring supplies to the Spaniards. Knowing that an eclipse was due, he confounded the Indians by keeping his word. From then on they paid homage to Columbus, their new deity, and he and his crew remained in good condition until Mendez finally returned with a fully equipped ship. On

Independent Picture Service

In the early part of the twentieth century, archaeological digs to unearth Arawak relics were undertaken by New York's Museum of the American Indian.

June 28, 1504, Columbus left Jamaica. Two years later he died in Spain.

Colonization

The search for gold continued despite Columbus's failure to find it. His son Diego Columbus—who was sent to Hispaniola in 1509 as governor general—sent Juan de Esquivel to Jamaica to form a colony. This date marked the beginning of the end for the Arawaks. Unused to the manual labor cruelly forced on them by the Spanish, the native Indians gradually died. It was reported that many of them preferred the poisonous juice of the bitter cassava plant to enslavement. Others fell prey to the illnesses that the Europeans spread wherever they went.

For years Jamaica was of little economic importance to Spain since no gold was discovered there. But its strategic value increased. The Spanish government urged Diego Columbus not only to continue searching for gold but also to develop Jamaica as a supply depot—by growing crops that were suitable to its soil. Cotton, a native plant, was further developed. Many new plants also were introduced.

Jamaica's coat of arms features two Arawak Indians, the original inhabitants of the island. The pineapples depicted on the shield are one of the country's many agricultural resources.

Among them was sugarcane, which would later become a staple of the economy. Livestock was brought in as well. Horses, hogs, and beef cattle became important in a very short time.

Many new and valuable varieties of sugarcane have been introduced to Jamaica. This one bears brushlike blossoms and lush, tropical foliage.

27

During this period of agricultural development the native island tree, the allspice, was discovered growing wild in the hill country. The berry from this tree is a highly desirable spice that combines the taste of nutmeg, cinnamon, and cloves. Today most of the world's allspice is cultivated in Jamaica.

With the extinction of the Arawaks, the colony of Jamaica faced the lack of a slave labor force. The island's only hope of developing into a first-rate agricultural colony for Spain depended on importing a work force to Jamaica. For a time, however, the colony was left largely to its own resources. Further colonization by Spain was not great—most gold-thirsty adventurers preferred to go to Mexico or Peru where the prospects were better. In 1611 Jamaican colonists reported there were only 1,510 inhabitants, of whom 558 were African slaves. This same report listed a mere 74 native Indians—just 100 years after Columbus had left the shores of the land of the Arawaks.

Spanish Days

Upon the death of Diego Columbus in 1536, Luis, his son, acquired Jamaica as a personal estate. He did not visit it, nor did his heirs. They reaped a small revenue from import duties and cared nothing for the welfare of the colony.

During the early days of Spanish occupation, a site on the southern coastal plains

Many ships went down off Jamaica's shores over the centuries. These relics were recently recovered from a sunken Spanish galleon. Although much copper, gold, silver, and brass are strewn around the sea floor, most of the treasure is too deep for recovery.

When the British captured Jamaica in 1655, they immediately saw the strategic importance of the island, and one year later they set up fortifications there. Historic Fort Charles now stands as the oldest and most important site in Port Royal. Named after King Charles II, Fort Charles had a lookout tower that was used for spotting the return of buccaneer expeditions.

was finally chosen as a capital for the new colony. Named Villa de la Vega, the site is known today as Spanish Town. Very few of the original structures of this settlement survive because they were built mostly of wood. Indeed, the Spanish left few visible marks on Jamaica, despite 150 years of occupation.

Under Spain, Jamaica was a neglected island. Occasionally it was visited by the English, notably Sir Anthony Shirley, who arrived in Spanish Town in 1597, and by French pirates who made periodic forays. Because the island was poor and fraught with petty feuds, it was easy prey for future conquerors.

The English

Before the English were to prevail, the French took a hand in pillaging Jamaica, beginning in the 1530s. By 1555 French privateers had swashbuckled their way into Negril Harbour on the very western tip of the island and had destroyed 15 Spanish galleons. At the same time, the famous English privateers—Sir Francis Drake, Sir John Hawkins, and Sir Anthony Shirley—were operating in the Caribbean.

When Shirley sailed into Jamaica, he sacked Villa de la Vega and happily sailed out again declaring it a "marvelous fertile isle," having met only feeble resistance from the Spanish. The English privateers state of Pennsylvania—and General Robert Venables, a British armada set out for Hispaniola. Defeated there, they next chose nearby Jamaica because it was poorly populated and weakly defended. Sailing into Kingston Harbour, they dispersed the defenders at Passage Fort after just a few shots. The Spanish fled and the British took over Jamaica, beginning a rule that was to last for more than 300 years.

The first British settlers were a varied lot—soldiers, prisoners, and drafted Irish. They had as their new governor Colonel Edward D'Oyley, who was appointed in 1661. Plagued by lazy colonists as well as by pestilence, the island did not develop as it might have. By the end of the seventeenth century Jamaica was a rollicking pirate base, with Port Royal at its heart. From here Henry Morgan, most famous of the Caribbean buccaneers, staged his marauding raids. He went on to become lieutenant governor.

Independent Picture Service

This eighteenth-century print portrays the taking of Jamaica by a joint army-navy force headed by Admiral William Penn and General Robert Venables. Sailing into Kingston Harbour in 1655, Penn and Venables quickly routed the Spanish and established Britain as the ruler of Jamaica.

were commissioned by the English crown to seize the commerce and war vessels of the enemy. They differed in this sense from the later freebooters and buccaneers who, as highway robbers of the sea, claimed all booty for themselves.

Such commissioned forays, however, were insignificant alongside the final invasion by the British in 1655, when Oliver Cromwell, Lord Protector of England, launched his Western Design—a plan to establish British rule over all of the Caribbean. Under the command of Admiral William Penn—father of the founder of the

Independent Picture Service

The uncrowned king of Port Royal and leader of all the buccaneers, Henry Morgan began his career with daring raids on Spanish towns. His most famous exploit was the sacking and burning of Panama City in 1671. Later, Morgan became lieutenant governor of Jamaica and eventually hanged some of the men who had sailed with him.

Port Royal under the British quickly developed into a rich and thriving pirate headquarters. The big-spending buccaneers, called the "Brethren of the Coast," created an atmosphere of revelry and debauchery, where law and order had no place. Drunkenness, gambling, duels, and vices of all kinds were common, and Port Royal came to be known as the "wickedest city on the earth."

A gift from Henry Morgan, the silver communion service used at Saint Peter's Church in Port Royal is believed to be part of the pirate's Panama loot.

The monumental, three-story ruins of Colbeck Castle lie northwest of Old Harbour. Although the castle's exact purpose and origin remain uncertain, it was possibly built as a plantation great house during the seventeenth century. With a massive square tower at each of its four corners and with connecting arched arcades, the house could easily have been transformed into a fort—which in those days was often necessary at a moment's notice.

Port Royal died as it lived—violently. In 1692 a great earthquake destroyed the town. This tombstone describes the unusual escape of Lewis Galdy, who "was swallowed up in the Great Earth-quake in the Year 1692 and by the Providence of God was by another Shock thrown into the Sea and Miraculously Saved."

The Eighteenth Century

During the sixteenth century England had pitted itself against Spain for control of the Caribbean. Britain was soon faced with another adversary—France. More or less continually, Britain and France vied for position in the West Indies during the seventeenth century. Throughout the eighteenth century, however, the British government in Jamaica busily developed the colony as a rich source of revenue through its sugar production.

THE SLAVE TRADE

During the eighteenth century well over 600,000 slaves were brought to Jamaica from Africa. The Sugar Act of 1739 provided for sugar from the West Indies to be shipped directly to Europe without having to pass through Britain. This made Jamaican sugar production even more attractive to investors, and the slave trade consequently increased.

Jamaican planters and landowners did not spend their whole lives on the tropical island. Houses rarely reached the grand proportions of the plantation houses on other islands. Landowners in Jamaica generally led a degenerate and gluttonous life, taking what there was to take and investing little in the long-term improvement of the land. Many seventeenth- and eighteenth-century visitors to the Caribbean islands—notably Lady Nugent, whose observations were many and well-recorded —remarked on the monumental intake of food and wine in Jamaica.

Absentee owners, often motivated only by greed, tolerated abuse of slaves by their resident managers. Although there were exceptions, Jamaica was infamous for its treatment of slaves. Many of them managed to escape to the remote hills of the island, where slaves of the Spanish had fled during the British capture of Jamaica in 1655. The fugitive slaves came to be

Piracy continued in Jamaica throughout the early years of the eighteenth century. Ann Bonney and Mary Read disguised themselves as men and fought with bloodthirsty fierceness with the crew of Calico Jack Rackham. The three were convicted of piracy at a trial in 1720.

Many Jamaican slaves were filled with a strong desire to rebel. This eighteenth-century painting depicts the Maroons in ambush on an estate in the parish of Trelawney. Most fugitive slaves escaped into the wild, unexplored hills where they formed Maroon settlements.

33

Greatest of the Maroon leaders, Cudjoe *(center)* is depicted here meeting in peace with an emissary of the British government in the late 1730s. One of many runaway slaves, Cudjoe had led the Clarendon Maroon bands in guerrilla warfare against the British settlers for over 40 years. By 1739 several peace treaties granted the Maroons 1,500 acres of land, as well as certain freedoms. Cudjoe became chief of his community for life, and he remains a legendary figure to this day.

known as Maroons from the Spanish word *cimarron*, meaning "wild or untamed." The slaves joined together in creating Maroon settlements, which still exist.

One such settlement, Accompong, is one of the few remaining vestiges of the Maroons. Along with a small band of Spanish soldiers, they fought against the British for many years. Peace treaties, which gave the Maroons land and established irrevocably their right to govern themselves, were finally granted in 1739.

The racial heritage of the Maroons is uncertain, but they are thought to descend from the great warrior tribes of Africa. They may be related to the Asante and Fante tribes of Africa's Gold Coast, who were noted for being particularly warlike. Slaves ranged from gentle to aggressive, and their physical characteristics, traditions, folklore, and customs varied considerably.

In 1774 the Jamaican House of Assembly sought to put a halt to the importation of slaves, but the attempt was violently resisted by those with British interests. By 1807, however, the trade had been stopped.

Accompong, on the edge of Cockpit Country, is named after the brother of the Maroon chief, Cudjoe. Here, Maroons are gathered to watch a dramatic presentation. Accompong is now the only Maroon village left on the western side of Jamaica.

Spanish Town, originally Villa de la Vega, was the capital of Jamaica from Spanish days until 1872. Once the scene of great gaiety and grandeur, its beautiful square includes the Rodney Memorial—built to honor the British naval hero Admiral George Rodney, who saved the island from capture by a French fleet in 1782.

When the British conquered Jamaica in 1655, most of the Spanish buildings at the present location of Spanish Town were destroyed, but their foundations were reused to erect structures more to British liking. Now housing local government offices, the Old House of Assembly, built by the British in 1762, has been greatly altered and restored.

Courtesy of Organization of American States

A poinciana tree, in seed stage, twists skyward in front of the Saint James Parish Church in Annotto Bay on the north coast. The church is a splendid example of eighteenth-century church architecture in Jamaica. Built between 1775 and 1782, it was dedicated to Saint James the Greater, patron saint of Spain. Although the church was destroyed by an earthquake in 1957, it has been faithfully restored.

The Nineteenth Century

The movement toward freedom in late eighteenth-century Europe was to have a profound effect on the distant colony of Jamaica—on both its people and its economy. As a plantation society dependent upon slavery for its prosperity, the colony's whole future seemed at stake when abolitionists—antislave activists—spoke out. The first warning of coming economic disaster appeared in 1823 when the British House of Commons passed a resolution providing for the gradual ending of slavery in the British colonies.

SLAVE REVOLT

After the abolition of the slave trade in 1807, the Jamaican slaves became increasingly aware of the promise of freedom. Shortly after Christmas in 1831, a full-scale slave rebellion began with fires at Montego Bay. Occasional but steady clashes between militia and slaves fol-

Courtesy of Museum of Modern Art of Latin America

Many artists and writers have come to work and live in Jamaica. This landscape of a waterfall near Kingston is the work of Joseph Bartholomew Kidd, a Scotsman who lived on the island from 1838 to 1840.

In 1838 Jamaican slaves achieved full independence, but freedom was hard-earned. They fought slowly and steadily for years – occasionally with a dramatic demonstration such as this burning of the Roehampton estate in 1832.

lowed, until emancipation was finally guaranteed. An 1833 law granted limited freedom beginning in 1834 and absolute freedom for all slaves by 1838.

A new era dawned. Former slaves became citizens of Jamaica, entitled to enjoy the same civil and political rights as white planters. But actual changes were slower to develop. At the time of the rebellion, the government and politics generally were dominated by a small but powerful group —planters of both white and mixed black-and-white parentage. During the next 30 years things did not change much. The same group retained control, and the former slaves were in a never-ending state of poverty made worse by taxation—a bitter by-product of freedom. When the former slaves appealed to Britain's Queen Victoria in 1865, she refused to give them any aid.

THE MORANT BAY REBELLION

Longstanding grievances between the poor black population and the repressive authorities within local government came to a head in Morant Bay. On October 11,

1865, a fierce massacre occurred in Jamaica. The Morant Bay courthouse—a symbol of oppression and injustice—was burned to the ground and 19 whites were killed. At least 354 people were executed, and many more were killed when the governor, Edward Eyre, declared martial law. Among the Jamaican heroes whose names are memorably engraved in local annals are those of the martyred George William Gordon and Paul Bogle—who were leaders of the insurrection.

A royal commission from Great Britain conducted hearings, and, as a result, Governor Eyre was removed from office. In 1866 the status of Jamaica changed to that of a crown colony. Although this meant that Jamaica lost some of its self-government to the British crown, many steps were taken to improve the social and economic lives of the people.

CROWN COLONY

Under its new status as a crown colony, Jamaica would become efficiently administered and economically prosperous. The first governor, Sir John Peter

Located on the square in Spanish Town, Old King's House served as the residence for the British governor from 1802 until 1872, when the capital was transferred to Kingston. In 1925 a fire destroyed much of the interior of the building.

Grant, helped initiate many reforms—principally upgrading the court system and granting land to the lower classes. In 1872 the capital was moved from Spanish Town to Kingston, and less-effective men succeeded Grant.

Blacks were entitled to elect anyone to office, and at the end of the nineteenth century a black person was finally placed in a high position. From that time on, blacks were assured a place in government.

In 1870 the future of Jamaica was enhanced by the discovery that the banana, a local product, had great potential as an export item. Captain Lorenzo Baker, a New England shipmaster, founded the banana company that was to become the United Fruit Company—the largest shipper of bananas in the West Indies and Latin America. Consequently, Jamaica was no longer solely dependent upon sugar. The expanding banana industry—both cultivation and exportation—added employment and income for many Jamaicans. An era of economic growth began in Jamaica and lasted nearly half a century.

Emergence as an Independent Nation

During the early years of the twentieth century, Jamaica remained relatively tran-quil. The greatest disturbances were those caused by nature—several serious hurricanes and an earthquake did much damage to the fruit and sugar plantations, as well as to many towns and cities.

In the 1930s a deadly blight nearly destroyed the banana industry and proved a serious blow to the Jamaican economy. General dissatisfaction with social and economic conditions led, once again, to social unrest and violence. Riots broke out in 1938. Two important political leaders emerged—Alexander Bustamante and Norman W. Manley. These men laid the groundwork for Jamaica's leading political parties. Bustamante founded the Jamaica Labour party, a politically moderate democratic organization that favored private ownership of the means of production. Manley founded the People's National party, a democratic-socialist group that favored state ownership. Both men were officially proclaimed national heroes on the first National Hero Day, inaugurated on October 20, 1969.

Although the outbreak of World War II in 1939 delayed political evolution in Jamaica, Britain finally granted a new constitution in 1944. In 1958 Jamaica joined nine other British territories to form the West Indies Federation. Three years later Jamaica withdrew from the federation and

In the 1870s the banana was discovered to be of tremendous importance to the Jamaican economy. For the next 60 years, banana trade to North America and Europe developed and flourished, bringing boom times to many parts of Jamaica. Disease, hurricanes, and the world war slowed the export market, but today the banana is still a major agricultural crop for Jamaica.

Courtesy of Minneapolis Public Library and Information Center

Independent Picture Service

Sir Alexander Bustamante, the first Jamaican prime minister, is chauffeured with Lady Bustamante. A hero of the poor and oppressed, Bustamante was a strong, popular leader. He founded the Jamaica Labour party in the 1940s and was influential in politics until his death in 1977.

Independent Picture Service

Michael Manley and his wife Beverly Manley stand before Jamaica House, where the governmental offices of the prime minister are located. Manley died in early 1997, five years after resigning from the office of prime minister.

—after attaining independence on August 6, 1962—elected to remain a member of the British Commonwealth of Nations.

Economic Development

In the 1950s Jamaica began an industrial development program. The government offered tax incentives to attract manufacturing firms. New jobs in the bauxite and sugar refineries were created. Factories were built to make textiles, clothing, batteries, paint, soap, and porcelain. An oil refinery, a cement plant, and a small steel mill were built near Kingston. Distance from potential customers, however, handicapped the growth of these industries. Subsequently, the tourist industry became the principal source of new jobs.

After People's National party (PNP) leader Michael Manley—son of Norman Manley—was elected prime minister in 1972, he raised taxes on bauxite in an attempt to increase revenue. As a result, Jamaican bauxite could no longer compete on the world market. At the same time, banana and sugar exports dropped.

Despite this decrease in revenues, government spending increased. The Manley administration sought to take over foreign bauxite companies. Manley decreased

private farm ownership, abolished private education, and heavily taxed Jamaica's business sector. By 1976 inflation had increased to more than 15 percent. The worsening economy once again affected social conditions. The resulting violence that broke out in Kingston reduced tourism, an important source of income. The standard of living declined, and smuggling operations became common.

Riots protesting poor economic conditions continued through the national elections in 1980. Edward Seaga, representing the Jamaica Labour party (JLP), defeated Manley in the election. Seaga's party won more than 75 percent of the voters.

As prime minister, Seaga emphasized improving agriculture and education, both of which were in great need of attention. He sought these changes through a return to several capitalist measures—private education, private farm ownership, and

Courtesy of Jamaica Tourist Board

Edward Seaga became prime minister of Jamaica in 1980 and is the leader of the Jamaica Labour party.

foreign investment in Jamaican industries. The National Family Planning Board encouraged Jamaicans to have no more than two children per family. Despite Seaga's efforts, the economy improved little.

In late 1988, Jamaica was struck by Hurricane Gilbert, a deadly storm that destroyed thousands of homes, important cash crops, and coastal tourist hotels.

In elections held in 1989, the voters gave the PNP a parliamentary majority and elected Manley as prime minister. During his second term, Manley adopted a program of economic austerity, limiting government spending in an attempt to lower inflation and lessen a heavy burden of foreign debt. Nevertheless, Jamaica's economic problems continued.

In early 1992, Manley announced that he was resigning his post due to ill health. The PNP then elected Percival Patterson to replace Manley as prime minister. In the 1993 general election, Patterson retained his office by a landslide margin.

The JLP accused Patterson of election malpractice, and in 1994 Jamaicans began demanding constitutional and electoral reform. Parliament initiated discussions about changes in election procedure. In October 1995, former JLP president Bruce Golding formed the National Democratic Movement, a political party dedicated to constitutional reform. It remains to be seen what kind of long-term effect the new party will have on Jamaican politics.

Government

A new constitution was enacted with Jamaican independence in August 1962. The British crown is represented by a governor general who is appointed by the monarch on the advice of the Jamaican prime minister. The governor general's role is largely ceremonial.

A cabinet led by a prime minister has the highest executive power in the Jamaican government. The prime minister—who is the leader of the party commanding a

Courtesy of Jamaica Tourist Board

Built after Jamaica became independent in 1962, Jamaica House is located on Hope Road in Kingston.

majority of seats in the legislature—chooses the cabinet from parliament.

The legislature, or parliament, is made up of two chambers—a senate and a house of representatives. The senate consists of 21 people chosen by the governor general, 13 on the advice of the prime minister, 8 on the advice of the leader of the opposition party. The 60 members of the house of representatives are elected to five-year terms. All men and women aged 18 and over are eligible to vote. Electors and elected must be Jamaican or commonwealth citizens who have lived in Jamaica for at least 12 months before registering.

All human rights and freedoms are embodied in the constitution. Therefore, the judiciary system, the police force, and the civil service are strictly free from any political interference. The judicial branch, which has its roots in British common law, is headed by a chief justice. The Court of Appeal is appointed by the governor general on the advice of the prime minister and the opposition leader.

Members of the National Dance Theatre Company of Jamaica perform for visitors from many countries at a resort hotel in Montego Bay—one of the hubs of Jamaica's tourist business.

3) The People

"Out of Many, One People," the motto on Jamaica's coat of arms, is appropriate to the country's multiracial society. While most of Jamaica's 2.6 million people are of African or Afro-European descent, Chinese, Lebanese, and East Indians have all contributed to the island nation's cultural heritage.

Health and Education

Jamaicans are slightly better off in terms of health and literacy than many of their Latin American neighbors. Life expectancy at birth is 74 years, one of the highest in the Caribbean. The infant mortality rate of 24 deaths per 1,000 live births is below the average rate in the region. In the early 1990s, the public health service had a staff of about 3,130 in medicine, nursing, and pharmacology. There were almost 5,200 public hospital beds and more than 300 private hospital beds.

Jamaica's population is growing at an average annual rate of 1.8 percent, which gives the nation 38 years before its numbers will double. About 34 percent of the people are below 15 years of age. The island has a very high population density of 600 people per square mile. About 53 percent of Jamaicans live in urban areas.

Ninety-eight percent of the population was considered literate in the mid-1990s.

Chemistry is a popular subject among students at the University of the West Indies. This Kingston-based university draws students from all parts of the Caribbean and has affiliated campuses on several other islands.

Education is free at most schools—including the University of the West Indies, the Jamaica School of Agriculture, and the College of Arts, Science, and Technology. About 14,000 persons enrolled in higher education courses in 1994. The University of the West Indies maintains a campus in Kingston on the site of the old sugar plantation of Mona.

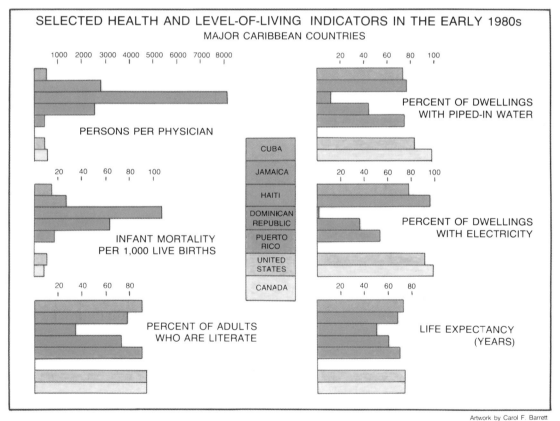

SELECTED HEALTH AND LEVEL-OF-LIVING INDICATORS IN THE EARLY 1980s
MAJOR CARIBBEAN COUNTRIES

1000 2000 3000 4000 5000 6000 7000 8000

PERSONS PER PHYSICIAN

20 40 60 80 100

PERCENT OF DWELLINGS WITH PIPED-IN WATER

20 40 60 80 100

INFANT MORTALITY PER 1,000 LIVE BIRTHS

CUBA
JAMAICA
HAITI
DOMINICAN REPUBLIC
PUERTO RICO
UNITED STATES
CANADA

20 40 60 80 100

PERCENT OF DWELLINGS WITH ELECTRICITY

20 40 60 80

PERCENT OF ADULTS WHO ARE LITERATE

20 40 60 80

LIFE EXPECTANCY (YEARS)

Artwork by Carol F. Barrett

This graph shows how greatly each of six factors, which are suggestive of the quality of life, varies among the five major Caribbean countries. The United States and Canada are included for comparison. Data from *UN Statistical Yearbook 1982, 1984 UN Demographic Yearbook, 1986 Britannica Book of the Year*, and "1986 World Population Data Sheet."

A delicate, silver candelabrum lights Saint Peter's Church at Port Royal. The church also has a rich, wooden organ loft, which was erected by ships' carpenters in 1743.

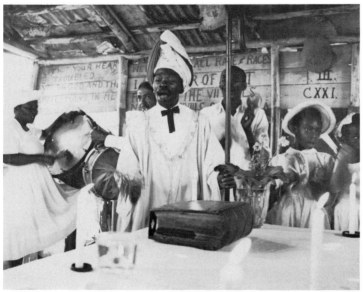

Pocomania, a form of Protestant revivalism, is popular mainly among poor and working-class people. Here, the preacher Kapo (Mallica Reynolds), who is also a noted Jamaican painter, leads a congregation in Pocomanian rites.

Religion

Religion plays an important role in the life of most Jamaicans today. Although the Anglican, Baptist, and Roman Catholic groups predominate among the established churches, there are many evangelical and revivalist sects, some with deep roots in African heritage.

POCOMANIA

Among these sects is Pocomania, found predominantly in Kingston. Practicing a form of revivalism that combines African beliefs with Christianity, Pocomanians believe that the spiritual and the living worlds are unified. Communication between the living and the dead is brought about when the living are possessed by spirits of the dead.

During Pocomanian services, a shepherd (male leader) or mother (female leader) leads the people in a séance consisting of singing, drumming, dancing, clapping, groaning, and praying that sometimes reach a frenzied level. A person possessed by a spirit might circle around, dance, speak in unknown tongues, or fall into a trance. Séances are followed by discussions, mostly about problems and troubles in the lives of the followers, or flock. After a person is fully possessed, the spirit usually becomes the person's guardian. The possessed person then consults his or her spirit on many matters in exchange for food or other offerings.

OBEAHISM

Punishable by law and practiced in secret, Obeahism is a form of black magic descending from African voodoo. Obeahmen and Obeahwomen claim to have the power to call upon spirits to bring about good or bad fortune. They make visits at night to those seeking their crafts and skills.

Traditional Obeah practitioners use only "bush"—that is, roots and herbs and other natural substances such as blood, ashes, bones, dirt, and feathers—in their cures.

A newer form of Obeah called "science" uses medicines compounded by druggists. These recipes may call for laundry blue, camphor, sulfur, and compounds such as "compellance powder" and "oil of comeback." Believers use Obeah in place of Western medicine, as well as to discover thieves or enemies, to ensure success in love or in passing tests, to influence court cases, or to get revenge.

RASTAFARIANISM

Rastafarianism is a modern religion with a rather loose doctrine that centers around a combination of East African culture and Old Testament laws. Although Rastas vary in the observance of their beliefs, they agree that Haile Selassie—emperor of Ethiopia from 1930 to 1974—is the black reincarnated Christ. Some also believe

Courtesy of Jamaica Tourist Board

Rastas form a partly religious, partly political cult whose spiritual allegiance is to the late emperor Haile Selassie of Ethiopia. They wear garments decorated with colors and designs of Jamaican and Ethiopian origin. After allowing soap to dry in their hair, Rastas work it into braids called dreadlocks.

45

A statue commemorating Bob Marley, the popular Rastafarian reggae musician, adorns Celebrity Park in Kingston.
Reggae music combines political and gospel overtones.

that Selassie is divine. The religion takes its name from Selassie's title before his coronation—Ras Tafari, meaning "crown prince" in Amharic, Ethiopia's principal language.

Rastas also agree that Ethiopia is the spiritual home of all black people and that they will achieve salvation when they return to Ethiopia. Finally, Rastas share the belief that *ganja* (marijuana) is the biblical herb and the means of communicating with God or of gaining insight or wisdom. Many let the locks of their hair grow long—called locksing—and listen to reggae music as an expression of their religion. In addition, many do not eat meat and do not drink alcohol. In general, Rastas hold humanistic values.

Music

Drama, song, and dance in Jamaica are interrelated and often rooted in the folk-

These young men participate in Sunsplash '86, the world's largest reggae music festival held annually in August at Jarrett Park in Montego Bay. The theme for the 1986 festival was "Sunsplash Against Apartheid." The festival has been held every year since 1978.

Courtesy of Jamaica Tourist Board

The limbo dancer provides a common form of entertainment in Jamaican hotels across the island.

Independent Picture Service

lore of the country. Recently, interest in native dance has developed throughout the island. The National Dance Theatre Company emphasizes the spirit of Jamaican dancing.

Although calypso from Trinidad has come to be associated with Jamaica and is played there, it is unlike the true native music. The sound of Jamaica's best-known

Jamaican musicians at a local dance (above) play a mento tune on the rhumba box and bongo drum. Although calypso is not native to the island, Jamaican hotels and nightclubs often pulsate with this lively music at night (right).

Independent Picture Service

47

This folk dance is called Plantation Revelry—one of many dances from the colonial period that the National Dance Theatre Company has revived in recent years.

Independent Picture Service

music—*mento*—is different from music of other Caribbean islands. This traditional folk music blends African rhythms with tunes related to English folk songs. The term *mento* refers to the words and dance steps as well as to the music. The words humorously reveal the folly of human behavior. Many Jamaican mentos are sung in dialect, making them difficult for visitors to understand. For example, a line from "Mango Walk" goes like this: "A warra dat y'u peakin', lilli lub o' mi heart."

Work songs perhaps constitute the oldest musical tradition in Jamaica. These songs originated among slaves who sang to relieve their toil. The rhythms were often patterned after the activity that they accompanied, such as working with picks

Independent Picture Service

The limbo is usually performed to a frenzied musical accompaniment. The dancer must bend over backwards and pass under a horizontal pole that is lowered slightly for each successive pass. Although everyone is asked to join in, only experienced dancers have leg muscles strong enough and limber enough to last very long.

As they spin a top, these boys chant "Gig lent, gig bite, gig dash away," which means that if the gig (top) strikes another person, that person may throw it as far as possible before play is resumed.

and shovels. Verses often alternate between a leader and a chorus, following an African tradition of call and response. Sometimes responses are sung by a chorus of people passing by on the street. Often the words are improvised. One of the most striking features of the folk songs is their carefree mood when compared with the mournful sadness of black spirituals from the southern United States.

In the 1960s native Jamaican rhythms merged with rock and other influences to create a distinctive national music called reggae. Although the sound and structure of this music was different from earlier forms of Jamaican popular music, reggae continued a tradition of using music as a medium of protest and social commentary —a tradition that had begun in the 1950s. By 1975 reggae had become popular in many countries, and Kingston has since become the Caribbean's most important music-recording center.

Folklore

While there is no professional theater in Jamaica, many amateur companies offer plays and musicals. At Christmastime, the Little Theatre produces a pantomime, usu-

ally based on the Anancy stories. Anancy, the oldest folklore figure in Jamaica, is a character brought from Africa by Jamaica's black ancestors. Brer (brother) Anancy, the hero, is sometimes a man but more often a spider with many of the characteristics of

Louise Bennett, Jamaica's principal folklorist, is a national favorite. Both a poet and a singer, she is unrivaled in her offerings of popular poems and Anancy tales.

49

humans. Through his cunning, the weak always manage to triumph over the strong. Such a figure was particularly satisfying to slaves who could not imagine triumphing over their oppressors. Some other recurring characters in the tales are Anancy's wife Crooky, his son Tacooma, and Asunu the elephant.

Another folk tradition is Jonkonnu, or John Canoe—a band of masqueraders who appear in some towns at Christmastime. The custom dates from the days of slavery, when the bands of masqueraders were much larger than they are today. In Jamaica the tradition became associated with Christmas, since that was the only

Courtesy of Jamaica Tourist Board

These children lead a simple lifestyle in rural Jamaica. The donkey—still the best means of transport for many people—is a familiar sight in the country.

major holiday granted to the slaves. Today the masqueraders may include a cow- or horse-head, a king and a queen, a devil, pitchy-patchy—an acrobat who wears tattered rags—Indians costumed in mirrors and feathers, a large pregnant woman, and often a mock police officer who keeps the motley group in line. Musicians playing a fife, drums, and rattles often accompany the band. The characters all wear masks and are played by men. They speak only in hoarse whispers to keep their identities secret. Jonkonnu is thought to originate from West African secret societies, and the word itself can be translated as "deadly sorcerer" or "sorcerer man."

Courtesy of Jamaica Tourist Board

Although Jonkonnu bands are smaller today than they were at their peak during the plantation era, the tradition continues. The masqueraders sometimes perform on stage, but more often they appear on the streets of towns and villages at Christmastime. Those who watch the players' antics are expected to contribute money to help pay for the group's costumes or to provide refreshments to keep up their energy.

Courtesy of Jamaica Tourist Board

Courtesy of Jamaica Tourist Board

51

Art

The earliest form of Jamaican art is found on cave walls painted by Arawak Indians. These drawings have been compared to prehistoric African art. Figures of birds and humans carrying spears and wearing headmasks have been discovered in Mountain River Cave in the parish of Saint Catherine. Arawak themes may have inspired Spanish artists who carved the ornamental friezes that adorned the buildings in Jamaica's first capital at Saint Ann's Bay.

Colonial art in the seventeenth and eighteenth centuries was created by and for the British expatriates. The heritages of the African slaves and of laborers from other countries were virtually ignored. Instead, this art used European artistic traditions familiar to Jamaica's colonists. Popular subjects included harbors, landscapes, and estates. Formal portraits were done for prominent families.

It was not until the twentieth century that Jamaica began to develop its own national artistic style. The social and economic turmoil of the 1930s generated a

search for a stronger national identity—one that would both improve the living standard and replace strong British influences. One of the leaders in the accompanying artistic movement came from the privileged class of Jamaicans. Sculptress Edna Manley—wife of Norman Manley—pioneered the break from British artistic style. The powerful wood carvings of Edna Manley capture the shape and form of native Jamaicans both physically and spiritually.

The most visually dynamic of the nationalistic styles is the intuitive, or primitive, art. Primitive painting has grown to include themes from Rastafarianism, as well as from both urban and rural life. In these works, Jamaican life is depicted with honesty and clarity. Some of the better-known painters include Karl Parboosingh, Ralph Campbell, and David Potter. Everald and Sam Brown have become known for their use of Rastafarian themes. Perhaps the most famous artist in Jamaica today is Mallica Reynolds, a Pocomanian leader who paints under the pseudonym Kapo. Kapo's paintings and wood carvings include lush landscapes and Garden-of-Eden images.

Courtesy of Jamaica Tourist Board

The wood carvings of Edna Manley—who pioneered the nationalistic movement in Jamaican art—have gained her an international following.

Mallica Reynolds, who paints under the name Kapo, has earned recognition as one of the world's finest intuitive (self-taught) artists. His canvasses are filled with vivid colors and lush vegetation. Kapo combines art with religion. He is dressed here in the clerical robes he wears as a Pocomanian preacher.

Literature

Like Jamaican art, Jamaican literature has also undergone a shift to more native or nationalistic themes in the twentieth century. Edna Manley, the notable woodcarver, was influential in the literary movement as well. Many Jamaican poets—still influenced by British topics—had been writing about snow and bitter winds they had never experienced. Manley encouraged these writers to describe Jamaican themes instead—such as the drought, "when the sun gets up in the morning and is king of the world all day, and everything is parched." As editor of "Focus," a 1940s anthology of young Jamaican writers, Manley helped to spread the work of nationalistic poets.

New Day—a novel written by Victor Reid and published in 1949—represented a turning point for Jamaicans both historically and artistically. *New Day* spans 80 years—from the Morant Bay Rebellion in 1865 to 1944 when the rights of the people were ensured by a new constitution. In his novel Reid shows Jamaicans to have their own identity, not as lost children of Africa or Asia but as people made by the island of Jamaica. Written in Jamaican dialect, even the language points out that Jamaicans are Jamaicans, not intruders from other parts of the world.

In the 1950s Roger Mais probed deeper still into Jamaican themes to reveal the slum dwellers living in Kingston. Mais combines a commitment to Jamaica's poor and working classes with an exploration of the strength of individuals. He insists that through inner strength individuals can find the resources necessary to overcome a hostile—sometimes even brutal—world. Mais's best-known novels are *The Hills Were Joyful Together, Brother Man,* and *Black Lightning.*

At Jamaica College in Kingston, students enjoy a beautiful, spacious campus with plantation-era buildings.

Jamaican homes often have many large windows, doors, and louvers —framed openings with fixed or movable slats—to permit the free circulation of breezes. Gingerbread, the artfully crafted wood trim, adds a decorative touch.

Food

At the time of Columbus's arrival in Jamaica, the Indians ate corn, fish, and yams—practically the only foods on the island. Since then, the native cuisine has become more varied, with contributions made over the centuries by newcomers to the island. The Spanish and British brought with them many fruits and vegetables.

One such transplant—the breadfruit—was introduced by Captain William Bligh in 1793. Bligh's first attempt to bring the plant to Jamaica in the 1780s has been immortalized in *Mutiny on the Bounty* by Charles Nordhoff and James Hall. Angry because Bligh had denied them water, saving it instead for the breadfruit seedlings, the ship's crew mutinied. The precious breadfruit was thrown overboard, and Bligh was set adrift in an open boat.

Many of the foods that were once considered slave fare later became national

Breadfruit *(above)*, which is usually baked, accompanies many Jamaican meals. The ackee *(right)*, introduced from West Africa, is one of the most commonly eaten fruits in Jamaica. When ripe, the large red-to-yellow fruits burst into three sections, revealing shiny black seeds and a bright yellow, edible flesh.

Jamaica's national dish, considered a delicacy, is salt fish boiled with ackee. Other seafood dishes are peppered shrimp and stuffed crayfish, lobster, and red snapper—often served with sliced onions, tomatoes, green peppers, and rice.

dishes. First among these is salt fish (cod) and ackee. Ackee, a bright red vegetable, was brought from West Africa in 1778. Its edible, yellow flesh—blended with salt fish, onions, green peppers, pork, eggs, and tomatoes—is served hot with its usual accompaniment, breadfruit. Breadfruit is a large, starchy vegetable that, like the ackee, grows on a tree.

Rice and peas, another traditional dish, is known popularly as the "Jamaican coat of arms." The special taste of this dish—a combination of red peas, rice, and coconut milk—is brought out by the addition of onions, garlic, pepper, and salt pork. For many Jamaicans, Sunday dinner without rice and peas is unthinkable.

Because of their colorful beauty, seasonal fruits and vegetables are the most attractive part of a contemporary Jamaican meal. Avocados, calalu (similar to spinach), chochos (similar to squash), plantains (large bananalike fruits), and yams are staples, along with pawpaws (papayas), mangoes, naseberries (a very sweet, small brown fruit), custard apples, and Otaheite apples. The Otaheite, a native of Tahiti, bears the old name of that island. Popular beverages include coconut milk, goat's milk, and mixtures of tamarind juice and soda or of soursop (a large, soft fruit) and milk.

Jamaica produces so much fruit that much of it rots on the ground. Among fruits that are unfamiliar to North Americans are breadfruit, sweetsop, soursop, and naseberry. The papaya (a large, soft, pear-shaped melon often eaten at breakfast or squeezed for its juice) and the mango (a yellow fruit with sweet, orange flesh surrounding a single, large pit) also grow well in tropical Jamaica.

Horse racing *(right)* **and cricket** *(below)* **have long been among the most popular sports in Jamaica.**

Sports

Introduced in the seventeenth century by the first English settlers, horse racing remains one of the most popular sports in Jamaica. Although racing was a sport of the wealthy, some of the best jockeys were slaves. No fair or agricultural show in Jamaica is complete without a mule, horse, or donkey race. Kingston has two excellent racetracks, which are always thronged with spectators.

Another sport introduced by the British is cricket. Founded over a century ago, the Kingston Cricket Club plays at Sabina Park, one of the foremost cricket grounds in the West Indies. Jamaica has figured in world athletic events in both cricket and track-and-field. In track, Olympic record breakers from Jamaica have included Herbert McKenley, Vincent Rhoden, and Arthur Wint.

In addition to these sports, swimming, bicycling, boxing, soccer, and polo are all popular activities. Most communities—as well as some businesses—support clubs that develop interest in competitive sports such as cricket and soccer.

Polo—a game played by teams who ride horseback and hit a wooden ball using mallets that have long, flexible handles—is another popular Jamaican sport.

Jamaica's largest industry—tourism—is centered in Montego Bay on the island's northwestern coast. This hotel is set in a Jamaican garden on Montego Bay.

4) The Economy

Problems familiar to many Third World countries trouble Jamaica's economy. These include relying heavily on a few exports—in Jamaica's case bauxite and sugar—whose earnings rise and fall owing to global factors beyond Jamaica's control. Like many former colonies, Jamaica entered upon independence with a people poorly prepared to participate in a modern economy. Many Jamaicans born before 1945 have never held a regular job or received the training that might have enabled them to be regularly employed. Many of Jamaica's unemployed have settled in the sprawling slums of Kingston—places that breed frustration and hostility.

Agriculture

Despite growing migration to Kingston from rural areas, about 22.5 percent of Jamaica's work force remains in agriculture. This means that available lands are often crowded, since only about 24 percent of the total area of Jamaica is suitable for crops—including some forested land that has been cleared for farming. Crop yields are often low because of traditional farming techniques and soil erosion on steep slopes. Many of the farms are smaller than five acres.

In the twentieth century, tree crops such as citrus and coffee beans began to replace the traditional crops of sugarcane, bananas, maize, and yams. Sugarcane and its by-products, rum and molasses, have long been Jamaica's principal agricultural products produced for export. Sugar output has been decreasing recently, however, because of fungus and rust diseases as well as mill breakdowns, bad weather, and labor disputes.

Other leading agricultural products are cocoa, allspice, and coconuts. In the 1970s and in 1988 banana growers were especially hard hit by storms that destroyed 95 percent of the trees in the main banana-producing areas. Farmers in the Blue Mountains raise a very high quality of coffee, most of which is exported to Japan. The illegal crop ganja, or marijuana, brings

Courtesy of Jamaica Tourist Board

A worker taps a keg of Jamaican rum at a distillery near Kingston. Jamaican rums are world famous and offer a wide variety between light and heavy tastes.

Courtesy of U.S. Drug Enforcement Administration

In 1984 approximately 14 percent of marijuana imports to the United States were grown in Jamaica. The island's mild climate allows some cultivation year-round, with peak harvesting in May and October.

Courtesy of U.S. Drug Enforcement Administration

Fruits and vegetables are widely sold at outdoor stalls. Among the foods unfamiliar to people from northern climates are green bananas and plantains (which are boiled or fried), chocho (a pear-shaped vegetable with a prickly skin), calalu (something like spinach), and cassava (a tuber that is ground to make a flour used in preparing bammy—savory flat cakes).

in over $250 million annually, more than the government earns from its chief legal export, bauxite.

The government—facing problems of a growing population, deforestation, and migration to the city and to other countries—encourages the training of agricultural agents versed in composting, crop rotation, and nutrition. Many of these agents travel from farm to farm, listening to farmers' problems and helping them to plant crops that they can sell to people in the cities.

A few large estates operated by corporations own 40 percent of Jamaica's agricultural area. A 1980 report from the Ministry of the Interior revealed that 21 families of British, Chinese, Syrian, and Jewish backgrounds control 104 companies. Many of these companies produce Jamaica's major agricultural exports—sugar, rum, and bananas—and have large

Jamaican coffee, carefully nurtured in the island's Blue Mountains, rates as one of the highest quality coffees in the world.

investments in electricity, banking, foreign trade, and natural resources.

The surface of much of Jamaica's land is mined for bauxite. As one of the world's largest exporters of bauxite, Jamaica ships the ore—most in its natural state, some as alumina—to the United States and Canada for refining.

Courtesy of Jamaica Tourist Board

Courtesy of Jamaica Tourist Board

Mining

Records of exploitation of minerals in Jamaica date back to the sixteenth century during the Spanish occupation. Before that the Arawak Indians used basalt, flint, and clay for tools and pottery. Minor amounts of gold, silver, and secondary minerals have been uncovered for centuries, and at one time copper mines were profitable.

After World War II, geologists began investigating the source of the red earth so prevalent in certain areas of Jamaica. They discovered one of the world's greatest bauxite deposits. Bauxite is the principal source of alumina, from which the lightweight metal aluminum is derived.

Nearly one-quarter of the island was found to be covered by this red earth, and, with the first shipment of bauxite in 1952,

Platforms allow trucks to load bauxite onto trains for transport across the country. Although a few refining plants have been developed in Jamaica, most of the dried bauxite is shipped directly overseas for processing.

Independent Picture Service

On a road between Kingston and Port Royal stands this vast cement factory, which throws a light coating of fine dust on everything nearby. The marl, from which the cement is obtained, is exposed on the hill in the background.

a new era began in Jamaica. Since that time, the country has become one of the world's largest producers of bauxite and a major exporter of alumina. The bauxite deposits are worked by foreign companies, mostly U.S. corporations. In 1994 almost 13 million tons of bauxite ore were mined, and in the 1990s, production of bauxite in Jamaica steadily increased. The country also produced 167,250 tons of gypsum.

A great interest in Jamaica's potential ore deposits has led to increased exploration by both domestic and foreign interests. Although bauxite mining was monopolized by foreign holders until the 1970s, the Jamaican government has now acquired 51 percent of the interest in bauxite. This nationalization has been extended to cover other sectors, including some agricultural exports.

Transportation and Communication

In 1990 the Jamaican government began a complete overhaul of the nation's road system, which includes more than 3,000 miles of main roads and 7,000 miles of secondary roads. The island's ports handle 13 million tons of cargo yearly. Commercial airlines operate through airports at Palisadoes and Montego Bay. Air Jamaica, a principal carrier, is owned by Air Canada and a group of local investors. Air Jamaica carried about 1 million passengers a year in the early 1990s.

Steady hands are required to solder jewelry, as this worker demonstrates at Sujanini Brothers Ltd., a Kingston firm.

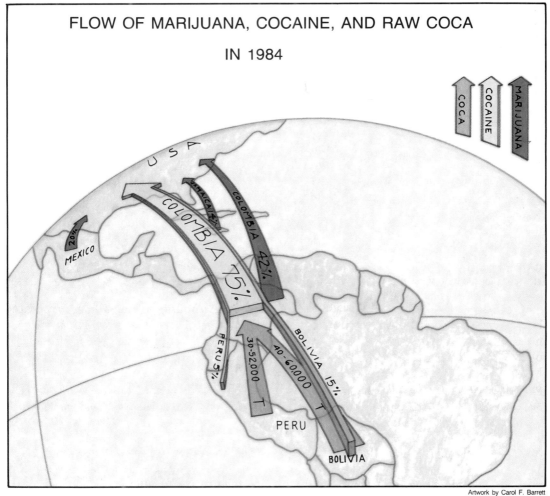

FLOW OF MARIJUANA, COCAINE, AND RAW COCA IN 1984

Artwork by Carol F. Barrett

This chart shows the country of origin and the percentage of total U.S. supplies of marijuana and cocaine that are sent to the United States from Latin America. Although coca is cultivated in Colombia itself, the chart also illustrates the movement of tonnages of Bolivian and Peruvian coca to Colombia for processing into cocaine. (Data from *Narcotics Intelligence Estimate 1984* compiled by the U.S. Drug Enforcement Administration, Washington, D.C.)

The Jamaica Telephone Company operates the telephone system. In 1993 there were 255,000 telephones in use—approximately one telephone for every 10 persons. Jamaica International Telecommunications, Ltd. (JAMINTEL) provides a wide range of international telecommunications services. There are five broadcasting companies, six radio stations and one television station. Jamaica also has an educational radio service that broadcasts during the school year.

Foreign Trade

Jamaica trades mainly with the United States, Great Britain, and Canada. Bauxite, sugar, and bananas are primary exports. Principal imports include minerals, fuels, lubricants, machinery and transport equipment, food, and manufactured goods. Tourism is one of the country's main sources of foreign exchange and is encouraged by the government. Owing to the political unrest during the mid-1970s and during the national elections in 1980, tour-

Courtesy of Kathleen Rosow

Castleton Botanic Gardens contain a wide variety of flora and fauna for nature enthusiasts who visit the island.

ism declined sharply. By the early 1990s, however, it had become the main source of income, ahead of bauxite and alumina. More than 1.5 million people per year visited Jamaica in the early 1990s. They spent almost $750 million.

Continuing Challenges

While much of Jamaica's economy has improved with increased industrial activity since the early 1950s, agriculture has not moved forward at the same rate. Before World War II, agriculture produced 36 percent of the island's total output. But in 1993, agriculture, forestry, and fishing combined provided only 8 percent.

Industry cannot yet employ enough workers to significantly reduce poverty and unemployment rates. One of Jamaica's most acute problems is rapid population growth. Overcrowded cities and schools, unemployment, uneven economic development, and underproduction are problems that must be solved soon if the country is to prosper.

The goverment is also attempting to stop the heavy flow of illegal drugs through the country, a trade that has brought increasing violence to Jamaica's cities. Although Jamaica has cooperated wtih other countries to control the production and smuggling of illicit drugs, marijuana continues to be an important cash crop in the countryside.

One of the qualities that many Jamaicans share is their positive response to adversity. Throughout the history of the island, Jamaicans have tried to better themselves when the opportunity arose. This characteristic may help the country to face future challenges.

Since achieving independence in 1962, Jamaicans are confident that their nation will ultimately succeed in forging material, social, and racial well-being for all.

63

Index